# IF YOU WERE A...

# Farmer

# IF YOU WERE A...
# Farmer

*Virginia Schomp*

**BENCHMARK BOOKS**

MARSHALL CAVENDISH
NEW YORK

*Dairy farmers raise herds of milk cows.*

If you were a farmer, you would live in the country. You would raise food and animals to feed hungry people.

What will grow on your farm? Crunchy carrots? Juicy berries? Tall golden fields of wheat and corn? Will you raise chickens for their eggs? Cows for their sweet, creamy milk?

All kinds of foods and farm animals keep the farmer busy throughout the year. Every day, every season, you would work hard in field and barnyard if you were a farmer.

*This giant cabbage is sure to win a prize at the county fair.*

*With the right care, seeds grow quickly into healthy young plants.*

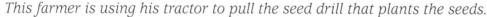

The last snow is melting. New leaves sprout on the trees. It's springtime on the farm. For many farmers, spring is the beginning of the growing season.

First the farmer plows the field. Sharp blades bite into the ground, breaking up the hard soil. Next the tractor tows the seed drill. Up and down the field, the drill pokes holes into the ground and drops in seeds. Soon neat rows of tiny plants will pop their heads above ground.

*This farmer is using his tractor to pull the seed drill that plants the seeds.*

*Airplanes may be used to spray chemicals on large fields.*

Just like people, plants need food to grow. Some of that food comes from the soil. The farmer makes the soil even richer by adding a mixture of vitamins and minerals called fertilizer.

Growing plants must be protected. Chemicals sprayed on fields kill the weeds, insects, and diseases that can damage crops. Some farmers worry that chemicals could harm the environment. They try to use fewer chemicals and more organic, or natural, methods for protecting their crops.

*Insects and diseases can damage or kill crops.*

Another danger to crops is too much water—or too little. If you were a farmer, you would watch the weather. Too much rain could cause flooding. Too little could turn your bright green fields brown and droopy.

Farmers bring water to dry fields through irrigation (eer-ih-GAY-shun). Pipes and sprinklers carry the water from streams and holding tanks to thirsty crops. In very dry weather, there may not be enough water for irrigation. Then a whole year's crops may be lost.

*These irrigation sprinklers turn like the hands of a clock, bringing a circle of green to dry cropland.*

*An apple picker fills her bucket with ripe, shiny fruit.*

*As the combine harvests corn, it spits the kernels out a chute into the farmer's wagon.*

After the long summer, crops are ready for harvesting. Apples, tomatoes, and some other crops are picked by hand. Most are harvested by machines.

Roaring and rattling, a combine (KAHM-bine) rolls down the field. This big machine harvests wheat, corn, and other grain crops. It also threshes, or separates the grain from the rest of the plant. In one hour, a combine can clear five acres of wheat—a job that used to take twelve workers a whole day.

Some of the harvested crops are sold. Some, like chopped corn and grasses, are stored in the tall silo to feed the farm animals through the coming winter.

Winter is a quiet time at the farm. Snow covers the roads and fields. In the farmhouse, the family enjoys the good foods grown last year. In the barn, the farmer cleans and repairs tools and machines. All must be ready for the start of a new growing season.

*An old-fashioned corncrib holds corn for winter feed.*

*There's always lots of noise and bustle in the chicken coop.*

Some farmers raise livestock, or animals, instead of crops. If you were a livestock farmer, you might raise cattle for beef, chicken for eggs, or sheep for their soft, woolly coats.

Some chores on the livestock farm are fun. You would enjoy bottle-feeding a newborn calf or lamb. Other jobs are less pleasant—like pulling on your boots to clean out the barn or pigpen.

*Sheep raised for their wool are sheared every summer and regrow their coats during the following year.*

*There's nothing like a good book shared with close friends on a cozy winter evening.*

Livestock farmers must keep their animals healthy and well fed all year long. In the spring, the farmer helps animal mothers care for new babies. In summer and fall, there are sheep to shear and corn to cut for animal feed.

During the winter, when the ground is bare, the farmer brings hay and grain to the livestock outdoors. Extra straw keeps barn stalls warm for animals that need shelter in bad weather. Some farmers even wrap young calves in coats so they won't catch cold.

*Cattle don't mind the snow and cold, but they need the farmer's help at mealtime.*

*Milking machines use the same gentle, pulsing motion as a calf nursing from its mother.*

It's five in the morning, but the cows are awake. And so is the dairy farmer. These livestock farmers raise milk cows. Each day they milk their cows at "five and five"— once in the early morning, once in the late afternoon.

Most modern dairy farms use milking machines. Pipes carry the milk right from the cows to containers that keep it cool and clean. During milking, the cows stand quiet and content, munching on tasty snacks of grain.

*Dairy cows file patiently into the milking parlor.*

The
farmer
adds
vitamins
to the
cows'
feed to
keep
them
strong
and
healthy.

*These bales of hay will feed the animals when snow covers the fields.*

After milking, the farmer cleans the milking room and barn, then gives the cows their breakfast. Now it's time for an afternoon of chores.

If you were a dairy farmer, you might take care of a sick calf or tinker with a cranky tractor. In spring and summer, you'd work in your fields. The corn and grasses you grow will feed your livestock all winter. Chopped-up corn is called silage. Grasses that are cut and dried for feed are called hay.

*Calves are bottle-fed to free up their mothers for milking.*

Late in the day, the morning's chores are repeated—milking, feeding, cleaning up. Everyone lends a hand. Older children help their parents take care of the crops and animals. Even a young child can give a newborn calf its bottle.

Evening brings the family together again. And maybe that's the best thing about living on a farm. Chores keep the farmer busy from morning to night, but there's always time for family—time for working together, enjoying a quiet moment, sharing the riches of the land.

*After chores are done, the farm family enjoys good food and good times together.*

*At agricultural college, students learn how to enrich the soil and care for growing crops.*

Would you like to live in the country? Do you enjoy planting a garden and taking care of animals? If you don't mind lots of work and early-morning hours, you could become a farmer.

Many young people who want to be farmers go to agricultural college. There they study crops and soil and the best way to raise farm animals. They learn that farming is a hard business. It is also fun and rewarding to farm the land and help feed hungry people.

*A farm visitor gets her first look at where a glass of milk comes from.*

# FARMERS IN TIME

About ten thousand years ago, the ancient Egyptians became one of the first peoples to use an animal-powered plow.

In the Middle Ages, the years from 500 to 1500, farmers loosened the soil with a harrow—a wooden frame with sharp iron spikes on the bottom.

Early American farmers learned how to plant potatoes and corn from Native Americans, the first people to grow these crops.

This horse-drawn reaper, invented by an American farmer in 1840, was the first machine for harvesting grain.

# A FARMER'S CLOTHING AND EQUIPMENT

Farmers wear comfortable, sturdy clothes and a cap for protection from the sun.

A computer helps the farmer keep track of work and costs.

This machine is called a combine because it *combines* two jobs—it harvests grain crops and it threshes, or separates the grain from the rest of the plant.

# WORDS TO KNOW

**agricultural**  Having to do with the science and business of farming.

**fertilizer**  A mixture that adds vitamins and minerals to soil to help plants grow.

**harvesting**  Gathering in a crop when it is ripe.

**irrigation** (eer-ih-GAY-shun)  A way of bringing water to cropland.

**livestock**  Animals raised on a farm for money.

**organic farming**  Using natural methods and no chemicals in raising crops.

**shear**  To cut off the wool from sheep or goats.

**silo**  A tall, round tower used to store food for farm animals.

**thresh**  To separate the grain from a harvested plant.

*This book is for Jefferson, Frederick, Ashley Rose,
Matthew, and Michael*

Benchmark Books
Marshall Cavendish Corporation
99 White Plains Road
Tarrytown, New York 10591
Copyright © 2001 by Marshall Cavendish Corporation

Library of Congress Cataloging-in-Publication Data
Schomp, Virginia, (date)
If you were a—farmer / Virginia Schomp.
p. cm.
Includes index.
Summary: Describes the activities of farmers at different times of the year and the various tools and machines that they use.
ISBN 0-7614-1001-5 (lib. bdg.)
1. Agriculture—Juvenile literature. 2. Farmers—Juvenile literature. [1. Farmers. 2. Occupations.] I. Title: Farmer. II. Title.
S519 .S34 2000    630—dc21    99-059658

Photo Research by Rose Corbett Gordon, Mystic CT
Cover: *The Image Bank*: G. Faint
*The Image Bank*:Michael Melford, 4, 12; Kuhn, Inc., 5, 24; Stephen Wilkes, 9; John P. Kelly, 15; Alvis Upitis, 20, 21; Eric Leigh Simmons, 30(top right); Lisa J. Goodman, 31. *David Whitelaw*: 1. *The Image Works*: Suzanne Dunn, 2. John Eastcott/Yva Momatiuk, 19; B.Mahoney, 22; B.Daemmrich, 26 (left); Wojnarowicz, 26 (right); J. Greenberg, 27. *Corbis/Digital Stock*: 6, 8, 10–11, 13, 23, 30(left), 30(bottom right). *U.S. Department of Agriculture*: 7, 16(left). *Peter Arnold, Inc*.: David Cavagnaro, 14; Clyde H. Smith, 25. *Archive Photos*: 16–17. *Index Stock Imagery*:18. *North Wind Picture Archives*: 28(top), 28(bottom), 29(top), 29(bottom).

Printed in Hong Kong
3  5  7  8  6  4  2

# INDEX